Coach Yourself To
A New Career

Coach Yourself To
A New Career

✦

A Guide For Discovering Your Ultimate Profession

Deborah Brown-Volkman

iUniverse, Inc.
New York Lincoln Shanghai

Coach Yourself To A New Career
A Guide For Discovering Your Ultimate Profession

iUniverse, Inc.

For information address:
iUniverse, Inc.
2021 Pine Lake Road, Suite 100
Lincoln, NE 68512
www.iuniverse.com

ISBN: 0-595-29658-0

Printed in the United States of America

Coach Yourself To A New Career would not be possible without the love and support of many people, especially my husband, Brian Volkman. Brian, thank you for believing in me and encouraging me to purse and obtain a career I am so passionate about.

TESTIMONIALS FROM COACHING CLIENTS

"Since I hired you after the 9–11 debacles here in NYC, you've been a godsend! After my business collapsed, I had no idea what I would do next. At first, I really didn't want to look at the opportunities; I just wanted to sulk. Thanks for gently prodding me to set a timeline and create a game plan. I love my new career choice. I do not know if I would have made it as quickly without you."

Michael Levin, Senior Vice President of Sales & Business Development, New York, NY

"During our work together, I have discovered that my true passion is to become a trainer and a writer. I cannot believe that this is actually happening! Surpass Your Dreams is a perfect name for your business because I have definitely surpassed mine."

Sean North, Analyst, Troy, MI

"I think every career site should have a link to surpassyourdreams.com. Your services have been worth every penny."

David Williams, Senior Level Publishing Executive, New York, NY

"Thank you, Coach, for believing in me, pushing me, and being my friend. Your support and affirmations have made a tremendous difference in my life. I still cannot believe the progress I am making. I feel like I have wings."

Jelaine Gilliam, Performance Consultant, Durham, NC

"If I had again the $1,000 I had spent previously on employment agencies, it would have been much better spent and been of higher value if I used the money for coaching with you. I hope your coaching practice takes you to great heights. You are a true success in my eyes."

Gary Woltal, Regional Sales Manager, Dallas, TX

"Since I hired you as my coach, I started a new job and have gone back to school. I have such a sense of optimism and hope for the future. My husband, coworkers, and family all notice the difference. I can't say enough about how beneficial coaching has been in my life."

Susan Jensen, M.D., Woodbridge, NJ

"Your coaching has made a dramatic difference in how I view and address the world today. I was constantly left in a place to be able to seize the day in an extraordinary fashion. You are a consummate professional and an extraordinary friend."

David R. Clark, President, DRC Advertising & Publishing, Stamford, CT

"I would like to thank you for all the positive changes that I've seen in my life since we started working together. After years of struggling with writer's block, I am happy to say that I am nearing the completion of a feature-length screenplay that I intend to shoot early next year. Thanks to you, I was able to overcome my fear of failure and rediscover the joys of creative writing. Now I'm experiencing total freedom around my creativity, so much so that I'm currently involved in three other film projects: a short film that I also co-wrote, and two documentary films."

Mario Diaz, Director, Producer, and Writer, New York, NY

Contents

Introduction

I'd like to accompany you on a journey that can lead you to your ideal career. Though the journey may take time, the only travel gear you will need is this book and plenty of paper and pens. If you're wondering about the fare, well, you've already made a partial payment, the price of this book. The balance payable is your time. My role will be to guide you throughout your journey so you will have the support and practical advice needed to make it to your destination. The journey may not always be easy, but it will be worth your commitment. The journey is about you, your career dream, and developing an action plan to make it happen.

My name is Deborah Brown-Volkman, and I am president of *Surpass Your Dreams, Inc.,* a career and mentor coaching company based in New York. The book you are holding in your hand is the result of my personal journey to find a career with a purpose, a career that would be my passion.

This journey spanned over 12 years during which I assisted and ran sales and marketing programs for Fortune 500 companies and dot.coms. It started when, fresh out of college, I got my first marketing job in Manhattan. It was the early 80s and Wall Street was booming. I loved the pace, the excitement of a big city environment and the high-figure salary I was earning. In fact, I loved it all. I was excelling at my job, but slowly turning into a corporate emblem. How could this have happened to me? I chose to work in marketing and sales because I was people-oriented, fascinated by how people behave, and wanted to gain a deeper understanding of what motivates them to take action. Yet, I was caught in a world that made no sense to me, where making decisions made an eternity look short. Day after day I took my assigned place, to work by rules created by others, for endless hours that belonged to others, to achieve the goals of others. I was slowly becoming invisible.

One blatant symptom that didn't sit well with the people in my life was my frequent job switching. They kept asking me, "What's wrong with you?" Additional questions such as, "Why can't you be happy?" and "Why can't you stay in one job for an extended period of time?" plagued me. I started each job with good intentions, telling myself, "This is it. I'm staying here forever." But a month or two later, I would start feeling unhappy again. For years I dreamt of a better way, but I had no goal and therefore no plan to implement it.

I remember burying my head in my hands and asking the universe for a way out. I got my answer three months later when I took a Learning Annex class on *How To Become A Coach.* During this class, I knew I had found my purpose. I had always wanted to motivate people but never thought I could make a living at it. The class was so compelling that my next career move made sense to me. Even though I was heading toward the unknown, I was ready to jump in. I signed up for coach training at Coach U and, in August 1998, opened my part-time coaching practice. For three and a half years, I coached clients in the evenings and on weekends while holding a full-time job. Then, in July 2001, I made the final break from the corporate world and set up my practice full time. I have been on a challenging and adventurous ride ever since. I have never been more content.

The interesting thing is that I don't think about switching careers anymore. I love what I do, and can't imagine doing anything else. As for the skills I learned while job-hopping—resume and cover letter writing, interviewing, networking, and salary negotiations—they have become coaching services I offer to my clients. Funny how things turn out.

The relationship I will build with you throughout this book is similar to the career coaching relationship I build with clients. It is based on my DECIR™ program, a five-step plan for creating a winning career. I created DECIR to enable my clients, at whatever stage of their career they find themselves, to take action to achieve the career of their dreams, in small, consistent steps. The five steps are 1. Describe What You Want; 2. Explore Your Options; 3. Create Your Game Plan; 4. Implement Your Plan; 5. Reach Your Goal. By following the DECIR steps, and the content in this book, you will have the tools to transform your career.

SO, CAN THIS BOOK HELP YOU?

This book can help you pinpoint your dream career. It won't tell you when or if you will obtain it; that is up to you. This book is about creating a clear vision of who you are, determining what you want, and using this information to develop an action plan to get it.

How To Use This Book

This book is based on a simple premise: if you can get your career thoughts and goals on paper, then you can define your next career move. To do that, you must first decide what you want. The rest is implementation.

You will find work tools in the form of questionnaires/exercises devised to help you develop the skills necessary to conquer obstacles in your career. Use this book to not only tackle your current career difficulties, but as a resource for the rest of your life.

Each chapter of this book includes writing exercises. Try to finish each chapter in a single sitting, but don't rush through a chapter just to complete it. This book was created to be a workbook. Use the spaces between the questions to fill in your answers. If you find you need more room to write, use additional sheets of paper, or consider using a journal or notebook to keep your answers in one place. When you are done with the book, go back and review all of the writing exercises. Ask yourself, "What do I know now that I did not know before I started the book?" Your answer is your next step.

1

Learning To Dream Again

o o o o o o o o o o o o o o o o o o o o o o o o o o o o o o o o o
"The future belongs to those who believe in the beauty of their dreams."

—**Eleanor Roosevelt**

Remember when you were younger and you *knew* what you wanted to be when you grew up? And how you blurted out, "I want to be…" to anyone who asked you? So why didn't you go after what you wanted? What got in the way of turning your dream into a reality? This chapter is key to bridging this gap.

In my coaching practice, I hear many clients say that they don't know what their dream careers are. Yet, when they finally do write their career dreams on paper, the dream seems clear. That's why my first job as their coach is to reconnect them with their dreams.

Let me begin by sharing with you what one client recently wrote to tell me.

"When I came to you two years ago, you asked me to write down what my long-term vision for myself was and this is what I wrote:

"I want to work part-time, or full-time, but with more normal hours so I can have two to three months off per year. I want to work for a multinational company that allows me to travel to Europe so that I can see my family. I want to get involved in nonprofit work on the side, as this is where I can really give something back to the world/community, especially in developing countries.

"I want you to know that the road has not always been easy but I am doing it all and I have never been happier! I am so glad that I followed my passion and vision. My job was so stressful for me and I realize now how unhappy I was. Thank you for being by my side as I decided to go after my dreams.

"I wanted to update you what's been going on with me. I am involved with nonprofit work. I am able to travel and have normal hours. I am able to see my family. Today, I am working in Ghana finishing a volunteer assignment in a high school. It is a great experience, and I am learning a lot. I recently went to Tanzania and climbed Kilimanjaro!!! I feel great. I have always wanted to do this, and it feels nice to have finally done it. I also went on a safari, and got my scuba-diving certification in Zanzibar, which was something I've been talking about for years.

"So, lots of changes. I am staying in Ghana for a while, doing volunteer work with a small IT company on its strategy and methodology. I am helping with programming in one of the rural banks here, as well as helping to open a farm by investing some of my own money to get it started. I will be buying an apartment in Galway, Ireland, that my brother will manage for me. I will be helping him and his wife open a restaurant down the road, so I have found a place to put my money to better use than the stock market!

"I want to thank you. I could have spent years talking about what I would do some day, but that some day is here."

From Niamh Darcy, former vice president of a Boston, MA Internet company. Niamh made her career move after she found the courage to leave an Internet company that was dying. She sold her home and went after her dreams.

What Types Of People Make Changes In Their Career?

They're women and men just like you. They were stuck in the wrong job and searching for the career they were meant to have. Here are some of them:

Randall Livengood who was downsized after 24 years with the same company.

Dirk, an architect from Belgium, who was burnt out, in a bad marriage, and ready for a change.

Jennifer Carlson, who was miserable in her job where she punched numbers every day. Yet she got promoted on a regular basis so this made it harder for her to think about doing something else.

Pauline Fleming, whose husband's company was relocating, and who was unsure she would find a job in her new town.

Valene Rayner, a 22-year-old college student employed full-time by an engineering company, who woke up one morning and realized that her life no longer worked for her.

Vicki Loveland, who hated her job because inside was a writer and singer waiting to come out.

Linda May, who had a growing sense of restlessness and eagerness, and was ready for a career that brought her meaning and purpose.

Do any of these situations sound like yours? If so, use this book to develop the personal power to make significant changes, to reconnect with your dreams, and move toward the right career for you.

Are You A Dream Come True?

Even though you may not be convinced yet, you have the potential to be. Consider the story of Todd who persisted in making his dream come true:

"In 1989, I developed a visual impairment that caused me to quit teaching. It got to the point that I couldn't see all the students at the same time, due to tunnel vision. I was too stubborn to let this visual impairment make me quit on living life to the fullest. I contacted the vocational rehabilitation office in my area and spoke with a specialist responsible for getting jobs for visually impaired people.

"One of these opportunities was a job through a state agency that specialized in vending machines and restaurant management. The first job I got was with a delicatessen that had a few vending machines. Previously, it had so many bad managers that they were ready to close. The customers hated the previous managers; they boycotted the delicatessen and tore up the vending machines that were there.

"I decided that I was up to the challenge. I worked with the managers and customers to make the situation better. We developed surveys that assessed why customers were so unhappy and implemented their requests. It was hard work, but it was worth it. By the end of the year, sales had doubled. I owe my success to a belief it could be done and a belief in myself."

If Todd was able to overcome his obstacles and find a career he is passionate about, so can you!

Here's another story of a woman who quit a dissatisfying position to find her career dream:

"I had an incredibly successful career: After being a director of marketing for a large multinational Internet company based in Italy, I realized that what fulfilled me up to this point (having an important job title, and all the success that goes with it) didn't fulfill me anymore. I was extremely unhappy. I wasn't seeing my boyfriend because I spent so much time at work. My blood pressure was high and the quality of my life was low.

"I decided that I needed to quit my job and reorient my life around my true values. I discussed my plan with my boyfriend and we decided where we wanted to live and what kind of life we wanted. Then I started looking for a new career.

"I came upon a coaching web site, and I realized that I could get paid for doing what was already natural to me—being a coach. I signed up for formal coach training and started my practice. I created a coaching company and my new Web site soon after.

"My biggest obstacle was that, in Italy, almost no one had heard of coaching. The only coaches who lived here worked for corporations while I wanted to work for myself. I created a press release to let people know what coaching was. I knew that once people understood what coaching is, then they would be willing to give it a try.

"The positive feedback was enormous. It overwhelmed me. I was featured in more than 45 interviews in magazines, newspapers, and on TV and radio shows. My monthly newsletter subscriber base reached more than 600 subscribers in a few months. I started the Italian Coach Federation (a chapter of International Coach

Federation) and convinced other Italian coaches to share and learn from each other. In four months, 30 coaches joined the federation.

"Before I made the leap, I was afraid to fail. I was worried what people would say, such as "How come you were a marketer yesterday and a coach today?" I used my coach as a resource to help me overcome this. She gave me the tools and the encouragement I needed. She helped me realize that I was already a good coach and didn't have to prove anything to anyone. I probably would have met only 25 percent of my goals without her assistance. My boyfriend was also a tremendous support. He's my biggest fan. He always acknowledged me and reminded me how good I was. I stay motivated by continually giving back to the coaching community. I can see a tremendous energy every time we meet or share.

"After taking the leap, I knew I was on the right track when I received an e-mail from one of my first clients. She told me that before we worked together she was surrounded by fog. Now she realized that she only needed a new pair of glasses. She said I was her glasses."

Every day we read or hear about people who are living their dreams, who are doing what they love. Are you? If not, see if any of these reasons ring true for you:

1.   You don't believe that you can live your dreams. Either your belief system has you thinking that you can't do what you love, or you don't believe it can happen to you.

2.   You aren't clear about what would make you happy so, rather than starting on any path, you do nothing because you fear making a mistake.

3.   You don't think you have a dream. Everyone has a dream. Some people keep their dream locked up inside and never see or allow themselves to find it.

4.   You're afraid of failure, rejection, or being different. Most of us are afraid of something. Don't allow your fears to keep you from achieving what you want.

5.   You don't believe you can make enough money living your dreams. This is the one of the biggest obstacles that keeps people doing work that they don't find appealing or exciting anymore. You rationalize, "The work is not that bad" or "I'm getting paid a lot, more than I could make doing something I love."

6. You think you are destined to have a less than fulfilling career and, as a result, you do not take action towards your dreams.

7. You don't think you have the time to live your dreams.

8. You don't think you have to put effort into your career, because what you want will fall into your lap.

9. You don't think you deserve to be happy in your career because so many people in the world are unhappy in theirs.

10. You aren't ready. Turning your career around requires a significant investment in yourself. You can do it only if you're ready[1].

Finding The Daydreamer In You

Now that you've started to think about your dream career, let's touch on the importance of daydreaming, using it to get an honest sense of your current situation and to guide you to the career you were meant to have. "Daydreaming allows your imagination to see yourself as something else, and once inspired, the motivator to give it animation," says Cheryl C. Helynck, business owner and writer[2].

Did you ever have a teacher that scolded you or someone in your class for daydreaming? I did. This scolding set off one major alarm—daydreaming is no good and a waste of time. Yet, since then, I've seen countless wealthy and successful people utilize the tool of daydreaming on a regular basis. Why? Because from the quiet stillness of daydreaming comes great ideas and the opportunity to hear yourself think. Daydreaming can provide precious insight into your needs and desires. Daydreaming is a useful tool for reaching your goals.

In order to daydream, stop all the activity around you. Try it. Turn off all the phones, television, and radio. Find a quiet place that's peaceful and comfortable. Sit down for ten minutes and let your mind go blank. Empty it of all your day-to-day responsibilities and let it go very still. These first ten minutes may seem like an eternity, but eventually you will be able to build up your endur-

---

1. Based on a list created by Susan Kennedy. Ms. Kennedy can be reached at coachsk@onramp.net

2. Ms. Helynck's quote can be found at whiteshadow.com/DayDreaming.htm

ance. Not sleep dreaming, awake dreaming. It starts when you are able to quiet your soul.

Keep a notebook and write down what each ten-minute daydreaming experience was like for you. What went through your mind? Did your mind race? How long were you actually able to sit still? Most importantly, how did you feel afterwards? Better? Great. You've just begun.

If you find that you simply cannot put your mind to rest, try writing first. Use a notebook to write down whatever is going through your head. Don't think about what you are writing about. Don't worry about grammar or how well it's written. Just write. Scribble your frustrations, anger, and disappointments. You will feel better afterwards. You will notice a significant difference in your well-being. And your mind will be ready to be still.

Be Comfortable With Being Uncomfortable

When you reach your inner self, you will sometimes visit places that are uncomfortable. You may experience sadness, anger, or guilt. You may think about past mistakes. No matter what your feelings are, allow them to surface so you can acknowledge them, grieve them, and then move on.

You are not alone in whatever mistakes you've made, and your mistakes are probably not as bad as you believe they are. For my part, I wish I had pursued my full-time coaching career earlier than I did. I wonder if I could have worked harder or found coaching earlier. But this is not what happened. I took the path I was meant to take until I was ready to take a different one. I have chosen to forgive myself and move on.

Forgiveness is important because it allows you to say good-bye to your past. Forgiveness is how you grow and gain strength. Forgiveness is key to discovering your ultimate profession.

Your First Writing Exercise—1.1: Getting To Know You

Please answer each question fully, in as much detail as you can.

1. Who are you? (Example: I am a thirty-two year-old married woman with two children, who works and never has time to think. I'm happily married, but unsatisfied with who I am.)

2. Do you have a secret dream? What is it?

Now, Let's Get A Bit Personal

1. What would you like to change about yourself?

2. What would you like to keep?

3. What are you willing to change?

4. What changes would you like to make as a result of reading this book?

5. Would you like to change what's on your to-do list?

6. What items are not vital and can be eliminated?

7. What items can be delegated to someone else?

8. What are your hobbies? (List them even if you don't have time to do them.)

9. In the last month, how much time have you spent on those hobbies? Zero is a number!

10. List your talents. Are you using them right now?

11. Describe yourself in complete and honest detail. Everything, the emotional, spiritual, physical, and social *you*. Write until you've exhausted every internal word you have to say about yourself when you are alone. Get it out, get it on paper. Don't judge yourself or your reaction to this exercise. Whatever you are feeling is perfect.

12. What did you discover about yourself? Is it old or new information?

Congratulations! You just completed your first exercise.

From "Just A Job" To Your Career Dream

So, how can you tell the difference? If you're working strictly to earn a paycheck to pay the bills, you have a job. If your days are filled with passion and delight for the work you do, you have a career.

Here is how some of my clients described their dream careers when they were at the beginning of their shift from job to career:

"My dream career would be focusing on the areas where I can find fulfillment and can make a difference in the lives of others. It has to be creative." Linda May

"My dream career would be working at something I'd do if no one paid me to do it." Dale Alvaraz

"It has to get me excited. So excited that I would rather work on my business than watch TV or do something else. Another indicator is when I can wake up early without an alarm clock and I am looking forward to the day." Alex So

"I've begun to notice what kinds of activities engage my full intellect and passion, activities that totally engross me, create flow, and produce lapses in time. I want to turn these activities into something that's exciting and income generating." Ann Jenkins

"I look around at the people in my company who are supposedly moving their way up the ladder, and I realize that for most of them, it will be all that they will ever have. They will probably be at the same company for years, and maybe even decades, while I will move onto other things." Sean North

"I have gone through a lot in my life, and I believe these experiences have made me open to others. I have excelled at every job I've ever had, but want a job in human services because I am extremely passionate about helping others lift themselves up out of whatever problems they may be encountering." Jennifer Carlson

Writing Exercise 1–2: Where Your Real Passion Lies

1. What was your secret passion when you were younger?

2. Why didn't you follow this as your career?

3. Are you willing to pursue it now?

4. If your answer is no, why do you feel it's impossible?

5. If yes, what will you do to achieve it?

6. What fears do you have about pursuing your passion?

7. Are your fears stronger than your desire to make it happen?

8. How long will take to get over your fears?

9. Is it longer than the time you have spent adapting unhappily to your current situation?

10. What positive changes would occur in your life if you changed careers?

11. How can you make now the perfect time for a change?

12. Why won't you let anything stop you from achieving what you want?

The more honest your answers, the closer you will get to your goal.

You Deserve A Career You Love

You're darned right you do! But how do you know what is a career you'd love? Start by determining how you really want to spend eight to twelve hours a day making a living. Start thinking about what you would do if you never got paid to do it.

Writing Exercise 1–3: Pinpoint The Traits That Are Important To You In A Career

1. What do you like about your present job?

2. What do you dislike about it?

3. What are your strengths?

4. What are your weaknesses?

5. What would you do if money wasn't your primary objective?

Then, Ask Yourself These Questions

1. When you think of the best careers on earth, what comes to mind?

2. Why?

3. What attracts you to these careers?

4. How can you use the skills you have today to fit into one of these careers?

Giving It Your All

Are you willing to do all that's necessary to get your dream career? Even if you are, sometimes the road to realizing your dream isn't the road you can take. For instance, if brain surgery intrigues you, but ten years of school does not, then being a brain surgeon isn't a real dream for you. The goal is to combine what you are willing to do with what you are passionate about.

Here's the story of Kelly Drury who left her position as a director of marketing to follow her passion, a career in holistic health. She is an example of someone who gave it her all.

"I used to enjoy my job immensely, but then I began noticing that my attitude at work had become lethargic and uninterested. This had been going on for some time, and I realized that being at my job just didn't feel right to me anymore. I was not in sync with whom I really was, and that there were other things that I wanted to spend my time doing.

"I had always been interested in holistic health and alternative therapies and wanted to have my own business. But without an education in this area, and with money and time already spent on a degree in marketing, I didn't think a career in holistic health was possible for me. After I got in touch with several people in the field who told me how to make the career switch, I decided that going back to school would be my first move. I researched different educational paths until I found a school that would be perfect for me, and I quit my full-time job so I could devote myself to my new career.

"The scariest part was not knowing how I was going to support myself financially. I was also nervous that I wouldn't have the discipline to start my own business. I had a conversation with my family and asked for their support, and they said they would stand behind me. My boyfriend also offered me a part-time job at his company so I could make money while going back to school. When I saw how supportive the people in my life were being, I realized that there wasn't a reason in the world to keep me from going for it.

"My first success was day one in school. I felt like I belonged. I felt understood by the other people in the program, and by the teachers.

"The only real obstacle I had was finding a way to fit in a part-time job, and the training for my new career, with all of the other areas in my life. Making it all work has been challenging but worth it. I feel more like who I really am every day. I am excited to get up in the morning because I know I will be learning something new. I am looking forward to the life I am planning for myself. I also have started to take better care of my health so I can walk the talk before I see my first client.

In five years, I see myself having a successful holistic health counseling practice or owning a holistic wellness center where different types of holistic services are available. I want to make a difference in the world."

Realizing your deepest dreams and desires makes life exciting. Imagine being able to create a career you love, like Kelly did. Those with a dream change the world. The dream is in you. Use it to begin your journey today.

Writing Exercise 1–4: Possible Career Choices

1. Write down the top five activities that make you happiest.

2. Put a checkmark next to those activities that could be possible career choices. Note: There are so many different activities that can be turned into a career. Use your imagination. If you love to garden, how about a nursery or a gardening service? Think about alternative options like the Internet or working from home to get your idea off the ground. Let your mind dance with the possibilities and your possibilities will expand.

2

Evaluating Your Career Path

○ ○

"The farther behind I leave the past, the closer I am to forging my own character."

—Isabelle Eberhardt

This chapter is designed to answer a very important question, "How exactly did I get here?" Right off you may think that you've had no special career path, that your life has been a haphazard, disconnected journey, or you may be able to trace your career progression, step-by-step. Either way, the exercises in this chapter will help you see that you have followed a path, whether you have chosen it or not.

The purpose of these exercises is to get you to do an honest self-evaluation. Some of the questions may be tough to answer, but they'll provide you with invaluable insight as to how you arrived here. Use your answers to understand yourself, your choices, and where you are going.

Writing Exercise 2–1: Your Earliest Career Concept

1. What did your parents do for a living?

2. What did they teach you about making a living?

3. How did you feel about what your parents did for a living?

4. What childhood career expectations were placed upon you?

5. Do your parents' expectations continue to shape your own views? How?

Writing Exercise 2–2: Your Career Concept Upon High School Graduation

1. What did you dream of doing when you graduated from high school?

2. Did you follow your dream then?

3. If no, why not?

Writing Exercise 2–3: Your Career Concept Today

1. Where are you in your career today?

2. What has kept you from making a change in your career up to this point?

3. Are you ready to move towards a satisfying occupation?

Go over your answers carefully. What do they tell you? Most likely it's this: that the foundation of your career concept was formed long before you began your career. Once this foundation was formed, it continuously shaped your career, often in ways that no longer benefited you as you got older. Once you are aware of the pattern, you can break it. With this in mind, let's look at how success and rejection have also had an influence on your career.

How Success Shapes Your Career Path

Success that moves you towards your goals is the good outcome you want to have in your professional life. Success that moves you away from your goals is what you want to stay away from. Learning to distinguish between the two allows you to pursue your dreams.

Here's an example: Suppose your dream was to be a schoolteacher but your parents encouraged you to apply to law school. Your acceptance letter represents a great accomplishment, something to be proud of. But, because it's not the direction you really wanted to follow, it also got in the way of your dream.

Writing Exercise 2–4: The Influence Of Success

Let's look at whether your career has resulted in an outcome that has been bad or good for you:

1. List several career accomplishments that you consider a "success."

2. Evaluate whether each "success" allowed you to move in the direction of your career dreams or away from it? Answer *yes* (moved closer to career dreams) or *no* (moved away from career dreams).

3. Do your good successes outnumber the bad ones? (Add them up.)

4. Did any of these successes have a negative influence on your career? A positive influence? How?

How Rejection Shapes Your Career Path

Even though we may feel invincible when we throw our hats in the air on graduation day, at some point rejection comes creeping in to spoil the party. Rejection happens to all of us. Some people use rejection as motivation to try harder, to fine-tune their efforts. For others, rejection serves as a wake-up call to make them realize it is time for a change.

Rejection is not only inevitable, it is necessary to your progress. When one door closes, another opens. Without rejection, you may be stuck in the same place for a long time. The following exercise can help you understand how influential rejection has been in your career.

Writing Exercise 2–5: The Influence Of Rejection

1. Think about all the rejections you have experienced in your career. List them. Separate the rejections into two categories: those that ultimately had a positive influence on your career, and those that had a negative influence.

2. What is the biggest rejection that really stung in your career?

3. How does that rejection still affect your career today?

4. Looking further down the road, how does this rejection continue to influence the direction your career is taking?

Learning To Love Rejection

Most successes come with a bucket load of *NOs*. For instance, Colonel Sanders, the man who started Kentucky Fried Chicken, received thousands of rejections before he finally succeeded in selling his famous chicken recipe.

When I started my coaching career, I had a hard time dealing with rejection. I got very upset when perspective clients declined to hire me as their coach. Only when I learned that they weren't saying *no* to me personally, but rather to hiring me at that moment, was I able to let go of my pain. From that point forward, I was able to be myself and not try so hard anymore. This is when my business began to grow.

Time To Move Forward

Your past is your past. There is nothing you can do about it now. I have seen too many people dwell on poor career choices or mishaps, instead of using their energy to pick themselves up and move forward.

Use your past as a learning tool that can help you put your present career in perspective. Use it to understand your career, not to criticize it or yourself. Use it to celebrate the steps you have taken as a rite of passage towards future achievements.

Reflection

Probably without even realizing it, you have begun to realize the power of writing. Writing helps you gain insight into your career. Writing is instrumental in this process, and it can be the catalyst that takes you to your destination.

While you are involved in this process, please make a promise to yourself to write every day. Even if it's just the answers to one or two questions in a given chapter of this book. Your reward will be clarity, knowledge, and internal understanding.

Writing can help you to clear out the confusion. Writing can help you celebrate and focus on your achievements instead of your failures. There may be times when you will have this book in front of you and wonder how to answer a question. This is perfectly normal. Begin writing, even if you start with only one sentence. Be amazed as the words flow and your ideas fill the pages.

If you find that you want to write more, get a journal. It can be a spiral notebook, your home computer or your laptop. Some of my clients use notebooks for writing in the morning, computer files for setting goals during the day, and special journals for winding down in the evenings. There is no right or wrong way to write. Use whatever method works best for you. Whatever you choose, keep something you can write on with you at all times. When you have a good idea or a moment of inspiration strikes, you'll want to capture it.

3

Gaining Inner Clarity

o o o o o o o o o o o o o o o o o o o o o o o o o o o o o o o o

"Your only obligation in any lifetime is to be true to yourself. Being true to anyone else or anything else is not only impossible, but that mark of a fake messiah."

—*Richard Bach*

Silence Is Golden, Serenity Is Priceless

Once you let go of what's holding you back, it's time to make room to hear yourself think. Silence is a great way to accomplish this. Embracing silence is powerful. It can help the outside hear what the inside has been telling it for years. If you already cherish silence as a secret weapon, you're very fortunate. If you dismiss silence as a waste of time, you've got a lot of company. We're living in a time of constant motion. We give ourselves little opportunity to think. When was the last time you had the opportunity to just sit and be still? I'm willing to bet that a thousand "busy" thoughts were scrambling around in your head trying to get you back up and moving again. We have become little pink bunnies attached to an endless battery stream that keeps us hopping long after we want to stop.

If your immediate reaction is "uh-uh, this isn't for me," bear with me. Silence is not about quitting your activities cold turkey, rather it's about learning to take time away from over-activity and simply stop and be quiet. With time, you'll get to know yourself in a whole new way. You'll begin to understand why you conduct yourself in a certain manner and connect with your own truth. Suddenly your intuition becomes keener, and you're able to steer your career in a positive direction. In fact, the idea to write this book came to me during a moment of silence. I knew that writing one's way to a fulfilling career was possible and that a book would be the best medium for sharing this process with you.

Here are some pointers on how to how to practice silence. Begin by setting aside a time in your schedule and finding a place where you can sit without interruption. It doesn't matter how big or small the space is; what counts is that you are surrounded by silence. It is advisable that you let the people you live with know what you are doing and why, so they can support you.

If you have a phone nearby, turn it off. Better yet, unplug it so it won't ring. If you are away from home, turn off your cell phone.

When you first start, your mind will whirl and play tricks on you trying to get you back into motion. Let it whirl. Eventually the whirling will stop, and you will find yourself in a place of silence. Let the silence sink in. Let your thoughts ride in and out, but don't concentrate on any one thing.

Start small. In the beginning, don't try to unplug into silence for long hauls. Start with ten minutes, and increase your "silent time" by five-minute intervals, until you reach a length of time that provides peace and clarity.

You may be thinking, "Will silence really benefit me?" Yes. Silence takes commitment, and it doesn't always come easily. It is a practiced exercise that you do on a regular basis, no matter how chaotic your schedule might be. What will surprise you is that, after weeks of practicing silence, you'll realize you haven't really missed anything. Your reports will still be done, the dishes will still get washed, and the bills will still get paid on time. But instead of feeling as if you can never catch up, you'll feel like you're in charge of your schedule, that it no longer runs you. It is a liberating feeling.

Writing Exercise 3–1: For One Full Week Take Ten Minutes Each Day To Be Silent

Before you start your first week, answer the following:

1. What will prevent me from being silent?

2. What system or process will I put in place to ensure that I have some silent time?

Writing Exercise 3–2: After Your Week Of Being Silent Answer These Questions

1. Did being silent work?

2. What didn't work?

3. What did I learn?

4. How can I apply what I learned to what I am presently struggling with in my career?

Once you've written your answers, take time to reflect on the insights they have provided you. Don't worry if you didn't take the time to be quiet every day. This is okay. Being quiet is still new to you. The very fact that you tried the exercise is praiseworthy. So congratulate yourself! (And be sure to commit yourself to the silence exercise the following week so you can experience the exercise fully).

Continue to practice silence, week after week. Let your heart have time to speak to your soul. Make being silent the best part of your day.

Listening To Your Inner Voice

One of the most precious gifts that silence and solitude will reveal to you is a quiet and wise inner voice residing deep within you. This voice can guide you through your career, provided you take time to listen to it. It may take awhile to hear this voice but, once it surfaces, you will know your internal friend is with you at all times, holding you back from some decisions, and pushing you toward others.

All of us have had a time in our life when our inner voice told us what to do. Maybe we ignored it, and something bad happened. Maybe we listened, and something good came into our lives. The following story eloquently illustrates the power of the inner voice.

"I was traveling down a country road, going approximately five miles under the speed limit. I had left town for some quiet time and wasn't in any particular hurry. It was a pretty summer day, and the drive was helping me to unwind. As I came to an intersection, I was suddenly jolted by the feeling that I should stop. At first I laughed off the feeling. I was literally the only person on the road, with no other cars in sight. I couldn't see the road merging ahead; the area felt so silent it seemed silly to stop. However, the feeling grew stronger as I continued down the road, so I stopped. Barely seconds after I did, a semi-truck (which was not legally allowed on this road) came barreling through the intersection at top speed. As I watched, my heart began to thunder and my blood ran cold. I started to shiver. If I had kept going, we would have collided. As I was in a tiny sports car, I am quite sure the impact would have killed me. It turns out the truck had lost its brakes and careened out of control into a nearby field. Thankfully, no one was hurt. From that day on, I always listened to my inner voice, no matter how silly it seemed."

Has something similar happened to you? Did things turn out well because you were tuned into your inner voice? When you allow yourself to listen to your inner voice, you have the power to make sound decisions. Trust yourself, trust your dreams. Your inner voice will tell you whether or not you are on the right path or not.

Writing Exercise 3–3: Remember A Time When Your Inner Voice Spoke To You

1. When was the last time your inner voice spoke to you? What happened?

2. What was the message you received?

3. What was your initial reaction?

4. If you ignored it, what happened?

5. If you listened to and acted upon it, what happened?

6. Do you believe that you have an inner voice or do you think life is just filled with coincidences?

Start paying attention to what your inner voice is telling you. Use it as your partner to further your career.

Finding Happiness

Most people want to be happy. This is a universal truth. Trouble is, there's no universal definition of happiness. And the media hype we get fed daily further muddies up our view of what happiness is. One day, it's getting that swanky new car, the one with the slim girl and successful looking guy. The next day, it's a house so big that, next to it, your neighbor's house looks like a shoebox. By now you should be so happy, but only after you have a house and a car payment you are under pressure to pay. Let's face it, advertising agencies don't care one stitch about your happiness. If you're buying they're smiling, but are you?

So what is happiness? Happiness is a feeling, and that feeling is different for everyone. It's what feels good inside. You may love to write and see yourself on the cover of a novel someday, but perhaps you also love to cook. Both of these are your pathways to being happy. The question is, which one can turn into a possible career choice?

The good news is you can be anything you want to be. The glitch is that this is both true and a lie. It's a lie because few of us will become rocket scientists or brain surgeons. It's the truth because, if you really had the desire to be either one, you could be. Since desire is nourished by your inherent abilities, talents, and drive, if you have no desire to pursue these professions, chances are slim you'll even consider them as possible careers.

Unless making money makes you happy, and you choose brain surgery because you find out that brain surgeons make a lot of money. Money may make you happy for a while. Maybe even for a long while. However—and I'm basing this on conversations I've had with many of my clients who have made a bundle of money who ask me, "Deborah, why am I still so unhappy?"—making money in a profession you do not enjoy cannot make you happy in the long run.

Money is the secondary reward for your honest efforts to pursue what is sincerely in you. This is a key point to remember. Remove money and its delusional effect on your thinking, and you can free yourself up to start down the path to inner wealth. Seems odd, doesn't it? Going in the direction of money for money's sake will make you miserable, poor in satisfaction. Going in the direction of your true purpose will make you rich inside and out.

Most people have a set of values by which they live. Use this time to evaluate yours. If your values conflict with your lifestyle, your happiness will be compromised. If you are working eighty hours a week but your value system says that spending time with your children is the most important thing in your life, then being away from them for long periods will make you unhappy. This is not to say that life isn't full of hard choices. Every decision, every lifestyle, offers a reward and requires sacrifices. It's up to you to determine which rewards will make you truly happy and which sacrifices you can live with.

Writing Exercise 3–4: Discover What Would Make You Happy In Your Career

1. What is making you unhappy in your career?

2. Has being in conflict with your values contributed to your unhappiness?

3. List one thing you can do this week to correct this.

4. At the end of the week, write down what you did and the results you obtained.

Are you starting to see what would make you happy in your career? Happiness is a journey of discovery. Don't rush it. Harried people are rarely happy people.

Using Your Creativity

Being creative makes us happy. That's because creativity allows us to express our talents and skills to their fullest capability. Nonetheless there are people who, for some reason, have convinced themselves they don't have time to be creative. And that's a shame! I ask that you put that notion away. You can make the time if you really want to. Especially if you realize how the lack of creativity is preventing you from having a career you love.

I know a publicist who is also a writer. Her schedule moves at the speed of light. In the course of her busy day, she regularly speaks with clients who have built multimillion-dollar empires. She loves what she does, but is the first to admit that, if she doesn't find time to be creative, then the day is lost for her. She goes to bed with a feeling of emptiness. It doesn't matter how many items she has checked off her to-do list; what matters most is having had the time to work on her book projects. She has learned that this is not fluff time; it is absolutely necessary for her happiness. Everything falls into place once her needs to be creative are met.

Like the publicist, I love to write. I write so I can express my inner thoughts, and be my true self. I love that my words, the ones that do not always come out easily when I am talking with someone, flow onto paper. I believe that writing is an important piece in how I will carry out my personal mission, coaching people to be fulfilled in their careers. I feel blessed that I have a career that allows me to be creative.

Unleash your own creativity by paying attention to the yearning feeling, the voice that tells you to paint, to write, or fix your car. These are clues to your little gifts of inner happiness. This happiness can be nurtured and you can help it grow.

Writing Exercise 3–5: Nurturing Your Creativity

1. Is there room in your life to be creative? If yes, why? If not, why not?

2. When you are being creative, what are you doing? (For example, writing, singing, painting, taking pictures, playing an instrument, telling a story, etc.)

3. What classes have you always wanted to take just for fun? How about taking one or learning more about the subject now?

4. How has not being creative hurt your career? How will being creative advance it?

4

Challenging Your Beliefs

In Chapter Two, you evaluated your career path and explored how different circumstances influenced the course of your career. As circumstances shaped your career, you began to form a set of beliefs that crystallized over time, until you could no longer imagine that they might not be true. The goal of this chapter is to help you identify the beliefs that are holding you back so you can challenge and overcome them.

Start by considering these three statements made by credible people—experts in their fields, which eventually proved to be spectacularly wrong:

"Heavier-than-air flying machines are impossible." ~ Lord Kelvin, 1895, British mathematician and physicist

"While theoretically and technically television may be feasible, commercially and financially I consider it an impossibility, a development of which we need waste little dreaming." ~ Lee DeForest, 1926, American radio pioneer

"I have traveled the length and breadth of this country and talked with the best people, and I can assure you that data processing is a fad that won't last out the year." ~ The editor in charge of business books for Prentice Hall, 1957

Imagine where we would be today if nobody had challenged the beliefs of Lord Kelvin, Lee DeForest, or the editor at Prentice Hall![1]

---

1. Experts Speak: The Definitive Compendium of Authoritative Misinformation, by Christopher Cerf and Victor Navasky.

Want To Know "The Truth?"

What you believe is the truth about your career *is* the truth—because you believe it. If you believe having a career you love is impossible, then this is your reality and truth.

Many people have negative ideas about their careers because of frustrating experiences or failed efforts. Are you one of them? You can change this if you want to. So how do you go about changing your beliefs? Here is my answer: whatever beliefs you hold, these are the ideas you have chosen to accept. To change them, stop choosing to accept them. Each time you hear yourself saying "I CAN'T" replace it with "I CAN."

Changing your thinking won't solve all your problems, but it's a great starting point. You'll still have work to do to achieve your dreams, but at least you'll be headed in the right direction with a good attitude.

Okay, let's do some writing.

Writing Exercise 4–1: "I Can't"

Think about some of your career-related ideas that you accept as true. How many of these beliefs have turned into "I CAN'Ts" regarding your career? List them now:

1. I can't _____.

2. I can't _____.

3. I can't _____.

4. I can't _____.

Writing Exercise 4–2: "I Can"

Take the "I CAN'Ts" from the previous exercise and turn them around. List them as "I CANs"

1. I can _____.

2. I can _____.

3. I can _____.

4. I can _____.

Do you feel the difference?

How Excuses Tie Into Your Beliefs

Your negative beliefs turn into reasons and these reasons are why you don't have a career you love. Reasons turn into excuses that prevent you from obtaining your dream career. Excuses may appear to save you from failure (so you won't have to be disappointed again), but they also serve as walls that keep you from succeeding. You can turn your excuses from stumbling blocks into a paved road.

Here are some examples:

Excuse: "I don't have time"

Reality: You have as much time as all of us have. Are you making the best use of it? What can you delegate or eliminate?

Excuse: "I don't know enough"

Reality: No one does when we start out. How can you change this? Can you read a book, take a class, or find a mentor or a coach to help you? You have lots of options available.

Excuse: "It could never happen to me"

Reality: Why not? It happens to people like you and me daily. All successful people one day decided to believe in themselves, to never give up on their dreams.

Writing Exercise 4–3: Let's Personalize This For You

1. What are your five best excuses?

2. Why do you love these excuses?

3. Why do you hate these excuses?

4. How do these excuses keep you from becoming the person you want to be?

5. Are you willing to let go of these excuses?

6. How will you turn these excuses from obstacles into paved roads?

Give yourself a round of applause.

Don't Let Discouragement Sidetrack You

We all get discouraged at some point in our lives, especially when change is upon us. This feeling is compounded when we fail to receive the support we need from the outside world. And the more uncertain we feel, the easier it is to adopt other people's negative beliefs and let them stop us.

Here is how some career changers have overcome discouragement and made their way to careers they love:

"Many people smiled and I saw in their eyes that they thought I was making a big mistake. Other people, mostly those who did not have their own businesses, told me that I should get a regular job with solid benefits instead. I handled it first by gently defending myself, and in hearing myself speak, I gained the courage and strength to keep moving. Other times, I changed the subject or walk away." Linda May

"A corporate retiree said to me: "Wow, most people I know keep a real job and do real estate on the side.'" When I first heard this, I was scared to death because my wounds were still fresh from my recent layoff and I thought, he's probably right. But then I thought: This is a test to see if I really have the guts to do this. I accepted it as a challenge instead of a reason to not move forward." Randall Livengood

"The only people who discouraged me were my former friends and neighbors. I handled it by looking at things from a multidimensional perspective and saw that the same people who were discouraging me were the ones who were unhappy with their work, their way of life, and they were feeling helpless to do anything about it." Rey White

Writing Exercise 4–4: The People Around You

1. Who are the people in your life who will throw cold water on your goals?

2. What is their motivation? (Is it to protect you or them?)

3. What will you say if they throw a negative remark your way?

4. What tools or techniques will you use to empower you and diffuse them?

Turning Problems Into Poetry

If you've got career problems, large or small, welcome to the human race. And if you're waiting for your life to be problem-free before you take action in your career, you probably won't live that long. So whenever problems enter your life, make the best of them. How you face your problems defines how you move through your career. It is the difference between not having and having what you want.

So, why not turn your problems into poetry? Others have. Accident victims, victims of trauma, prisoners of war and cancer survivors have made careers out of their individual tragedies. They changed laws and made a difference in the world. In May 1995, during a cross-country event in Culpeper, Virginia, Christopher Reeve's thoroughbred balked at a rail jump, pitching him forward. Reeve's hands were tangled in the horse's bridle and he landed head first, fracturing the uppermost vertebrae in his spine. Reeve was instantly paralyzed from the neck down.

Christopher Reeve refused to be a victim. He used the international interest in his situation to increase public awareness about spinal cord injury and now devotes his life to raising money to find a cure. He became the Chairman of the American Paralysis Association and Vice Chairman of the National Organization on Disability. He accepted numerous invitations to appear as a speaker including at the Academy Awards, the Paralympics in Atlanta, and at the Democratic Convention, to name a few. His compelling autobiography, *Still Me,* was released in April 1998 and quickly became a best-seller. [2]

Christopher Reeve made poetry of his problems. How can you make poetry of yours?

---

2.   Text adapted from http://www.fortunecity.com/lavender/greatsleep/1023/biography.html

Writing Exercise 4–5: Tackling Problems

1. Start by listing the problems in your career that are currently weighing heavily on your mind.

2. Which of these problems can you control?

3. Which of these problems are out of your control?

4. What can you learn from these problems?

5. How can you turn your problems into poetry?

5

How Fear Affects Your Career

"Feel the fear and do it anyway."

—Susan Jeffers, author

What is fear? Fear is an emotion experienced in anticipation of a specific pain or danger. Simply put, when we fear the worst, we stay stuck and we don't take action.

Fear is normal. We all feel fear at certain points in our lives. But when fear prevents you from doing what you love for a living, then it's time to get fear out of the way. You won't wake up one day and not be afraid anymore. Your fear won't suddenly disappear on its own. It's going to take work. Still, you can have what you want; you'll just have to go after it while being afraid.

If you're afraid, you're not alone. Here are a few people who were afraid and pursued their new career despite their fear.

"I was afraid that I would not be able to take care of my son, go to school, and have a job all at the same time. I succeeded because I told myself that failure was not an option." Jennifer Carlson

"My biggest fear was maintaining one business while starting another. I was a single mom and I had to put food on the table." Mershon Bell

"I worried that I would not be able to pay my monthly bills, especially my mortgage." Ann Jenkins

"I worried that my past would keep me from having a future I really wanted. I allowed myself to be scared, to ask for help, and to fail. I allowed myself whatever I needed." Valene Raymer

"The hardest part of starting a new career was not knowing what I had to do to be successful. I learned that the fear of not succeeding ends when you decide that success is about learning and growing." Dale Alvaraz

"I dealt with my fears by enlisting the aid of a few core people whom I knew and respected professionally and socially. I also got outside support from a coach who was not encumbered with any previous involvement with me professionally or socially; an unbiased opinion, if you will, to lead my cheerleading squad." Michael Bruce

"I was afraid because I had a wife and a baby. When fear started to set it, I shifted my attention away from it. I just reminded myself about my past business and was grateful that I did not have to do that anymore." Alex So

Putting Your Fears At Bay

Dealing with fear head on usually dilutes the strong hold that keeps fear alive. As scary as this may seem, facing your fears is the secret to getting past them.

As a writer, I face my fears each time I sit in front of a blank piece of paper. All kinds of thoughts other than what I am writing about fly through my mind. At that moment, it seems that the tasks away from the blank piece of paper are more important. I think about my mailing list that I haven't updated in a week, the clients that I have to send e-mails to, and the woman I met at a networking meeting that I have to call. But as soon as I start writing my fears of not getting everything done slip away. So the sooner I confront my fears, the quicker I overcome them.

Writing Exercise 5–1: Identify Your Fears

1. What fears keep you from taking action today?

2. How do these fears work for you? How do they benefit you? What don't you have to look at or handle because of your fear?

3. What is the worst thing(s) you believe would happen if you went after a career you really wanted?

4. How have you overcome similar fear in the past? How can you use this knowledge to overcome your fears now?

Visualizing Your Fear Away

Successful people who have overcome their fears began with a determination to not let their fears stop them. They created a clear description of what they wanted in their mind. They visualized this description several times before it became a reality. They spent a great deal of time nurturing this description before they acted to make it real.

Let me share with you how visualization has worked for me. Even though I've been speaking in public for years, I still get afraid. (But I refuse to let my fear stop me). When I'm at the front of the room, I love it. It's when I am getting ready to speak that I am most nervous. What if I forget my words? What if the audience doesn't like what I am saying? My fear drives me wild. However, over time, I've been able to reduce my fear level, and with each speaking opportunity I've been able to manage my fear better. The way I do it is by visualizing that people are enjoying my presentation because it has value for them. Because I usually score high on providing value, I try to focus on the success achieved at previous presentations. I know that one day I will be a fear-free speaker.

Now it's your turn. Begin with a clear description of what you want to obtain. Visualize it several times. Nurture it before you identify the actions to support it. Put yourself mentally in the very situation that scares you and then do the following exercise.

Writing Exercise 5–2: Staring Down Your Fear

1. Identify a fear you would like to overcome. List one you are ready to confront today.

2. Write down how you visualize yourself doing what you are afraid of.

3. What can you do to overcome your fear?

4. How will you reward yourself for conquering your fear?

Writing Exercise 5–3: Conquering Your Fears

If all of your fears were conquered, how would you be different in each of these areas? Describe in detail what comes to mind:

A. Spiritual:

B. Physical:

C. Career:

D. Financial:

E. Materialistically:

F. Socially:

Next, Take Action

1. While you are working to get past your fear, or are no longer afraid, what can you do to advance in your career?

Get ready to make your dream career real!

6

Moving Forward

I recently worked with Bob (not his real name) who wanted to leave his job as an executive art director in an advertising company for a career in broadcasting. It was a dream of his since he was a little boy. Although he loved advertising, he really wanted to be in an environment that focused on current events. When Bob hired me as his coach, he was unhappy in his job, and he knew it was time to take action. The problem was Bob didn't know where to begin and he didn't want to walk away from his skills, talents, and expertise, something he worked very hard to obtain. So we brainstormed and identified the questions about whether a career in broadcasting was possible for him. We came up with a long list and narrowed it down to Bob's top four questions:

1. What employment opportunities are there in the field of broadcasting?

2. What training do I need?

3. How much money can I make?

4. What type of person excels in broadcasting?

Now let's look at how we answered Bob's questions:

1. What employment opportunities are there in the field of broadcasting?

I suggested to Bob to go to the library to obtain more information on broadcasting jobs and how he could use his current experience and skills in his new career. I asked Bob to check job boards to further his investigation. His goal was to determine if he could use his current skills set to get a job in broadcasting or if he required additional training.

2. What training do I need?

Bob determined that he needed further training. I suggested that he search on the Internet to find out what programs were available, what they cost, and what job opportunities he could expect when he was fully trained.

3. How much money can I make?

I suggested that Bob use the Internet to search for sites listing salaries for various broadcasting positions. This would give him a realistic idea of what he could earn. His goal was to find out if he had to take a pay cut or would freelance or part-time work do to earn additional money.

4. What type of person excels in broadcasting?

I suggested that Bob contact people in the broadcasting field. Bob called, e-mailed, and wrote letters. Guess what? The people he contacted replied to his letters and returned his telephone calls. They told him that they were so inspired by his passion for his new career that they wanted to help him.

As a result of his hard work, Bob found a job in broadcasting at a local cable station running its advertising group. His first step was using his current skill set to get a job in the industry of his choice. He is also undergoing training to be a reporter. Once he completes his training, he will apply for a position as a reporter. He will start with the people he knows at the cable station first.

Writing Exercise 6–1: Your Four Questions

1. What questions do you need to answer before you start on your new career? List them all. Then narrow them down to the top four.

2. Which questions will you answer first? Prioritize them. Set a date when you will have your answers.

3. How will you get your answers? What is your plan?

4. Who can help you?

Making The Commitment

Once you have your answers, the next step is committing yourself to your new career. Commitment is very heavy-duty stuff for most of us. This is because we want a guarantee before we test the waters. We want to know that we are making the right choice before we act. Unfortunately, life doesn't work this way. First, comes the commitment, the hard work. Second come the rewards. So what happens if you do make a bad choice? Remember that there are no "bad" choices, only different paths you can take. If you do make a choice that does not work out, you will move on and use what you learned to adjust your approach or make a new choice. The right choice will eventually become clear. And, when you see the finish line, you'll be grateful that you didn't give up.

When I decided to live my dream as a career coach, I was apprehensive. I kept asking myself, "What if it doesn't work out?" In the end, I chose to make the commitment to become a coach anyway. Today, I love my career. I believe it's due to the fact that I was committed to making coaching work. I admit that I still worry sometimes, but deep inside there's a conviction that I'm doing what I am supposed to be doing with my life. The initial struggle was saying, "Yes." Once I did, the rest was implementation.

When you make that commitment, get ready to experience an "aha" moment in your life. Take it from these career changers.

"The moment I made the commitment, there was a feeling of 'Yes! This is it!' It felt right." Julie D. Raque

"What told me I made the right decision to change careers were the people who said I made a difference in their lives. I knew I was on the right path." Dale Alvarez

"I just did it. I figured it was all or nothing. I'm glad I did." Vicki Loveland

"The first success occurred when two of my support group members became involved in the company as staff members. Not as investors, but actual working staff of the company." Michael Bruce

What does it take to make a commitment? Committed individuals have several traits in common. They are:

1. *People who make commitments:* They stick with their commitments because they said they would. Words such as *maybe, should,* or *can't* are absent from their vocabulary.

2. *People who believe they can fulfill their commitments:* They visualize the finish line and believe they will reach their goal. Because their beliefs are so strong, not reaching their goals isn't a consideration.

3. *People who invest in their commitments:* They invest their time, money, and energy. Their commitments become so important that they rework their lives to fit them in.

4. *People who are passionate about their commitments:* Their passion touches, moves, and inspires others around them. This passion carries them through to the end.

Are you still stuck? If you are, make a list of all the considerations that are keeping you from committing so you can get them out of your mind and out of your way.

Writing Exercise 6–2: Creating An Action Plan

Once the commitment is made, it is time to spring into action. Use these three questions to create your action plan.

1. What do I want?

Write down your specific career choice. If you are still uncertain about what you want to do, stop here and keep working on Exercise 6.1 until you are clear and comfortable with your career choice.

2. When?

Specify the exact date when you will have your new career. (Guess if you have to.)
This will give you something specific to aim for. Look at this date every day.

3. How?

What steps will you take to make your action plan real? Your answers in Exercise
6.1 are the specific steps you will take to reach your destination.

Staying Motivated

"When it is dark enough, you can see the stars." Charles Beard, president Braniff
Airways, 1954–1965

As you pursue your new career, don't expect the road to be entirely smooth, as
there will be bumps and potholes ahead. This doesn't mean that you've made the
wrong decision. It means you are human, and as humans, we sometimes have

doubts. If you find yourself questioning your decision, or your ability to succeed, that's the time to believe in yourself to override any negative thoughts that come your way.

How can you stay motivated during the rough times? Read how these career changers energized themselves.

"I stayed motivated with the simple fact that I was getting closer to me. The hard way, the lonely way, the not very attractive way, but my way." Valene Raymer

"I knew that only I could get it done and I had to keep at it. Period!" Lenore Beck

"The same thing that helped me overcome my obstacles kept me motivated. I revisited the passion I had for what I was doing." Dale Alvaraz

"I envisioned what success looked like and I motivated myself to achieve it." Anne Jenkins

"I knew that my future and the future of my family was going to be bright. No matter what it took. I was determined to succeed." Jennifer Carlson, social worker & counselor

For my part, I've had my share of doubts over the years. I've asked myself on a few occasions whether or not I should be a coach. When I began my coaching practice, I wondered if I could really help people. As the years went on, I wondered if I could make coaching a full-time career. When I became a full-time coach and the economy went into a downward spiral, I was not sure my business would make it. I remember telling my husband that I might have to close the business. Around the same time, we took a mini-vacation, which renewed my spirit and my drive.

I found the poem below in a gift shop in New Mexico. I knew it was meant for me.

Never Quit![1]

By C. W. Longenecker

When things go wrong, as they sometimes will, When the road you're trudging seems all uphill, When the funds are low, and the debts are high, And you want to smile, but you have to sigh, When care is pressing you down a bit, Rest if you must, but don't you quit.

Life is queer with its twists and turns, As everyone of us sometimes learns, And many a failure turns about, when he might have won had he stuck it out; Don't give up though the pace seems slow, You may succeed with another blow.

Success is failure turned inside out, The silver tint of the clouds of doubt, And you never can tell how close you are, It may be near when it seems so far; So stick to the fight when you're hardest hit, It's when things seem worse, that...

You Must Not Quit.

There will be times when you will question yourself and wonder why you are pursuing your path into the unknown. Questioning is good. Stopping and not fulfilling your destiny is unacceptable.

---

1.   Poem can be found at www.cyber-nation.com/victory/youcandoit/never_quit.htm

7

Implementing Your Plan

o o o o o o o o o o o o o o o o o o o o o o o o o o o o o o o

"Take time to deliberate, but when the time for action has arrived, stop thinking and go in."

—*Napoleon Bonaparte*

So far, you've done a great job evaluating your career, identifying your strengths, weaknesses, wishes, and those elements you no longer want to be part of your career. You've put together a plan. Now comes the effort to put it all into motion. Don't worry if you're feeling scared, even really scared. You can do this.

Writing Exercise 7–1: Break Down Your Plan From Exercise 6–2 Even Further

1. Working backwards from the date when you want to be in your new career, what do you need to do monthly to reach your goal?

2. Working backwards, what do you need to do weekly to reach your goal?

3. Working backwards, what do you need to do daily to reach your goal?

4. Whom will you enlist to support you in making your plan happen?

5. What method will you use to keep track of your progress? Paper or electronic?

Writing Exercise 7–2: Identify The Additional Resources You'll Need To Support New Career Choice

1. What do you still need to do before you can make your transition?

2. Who can help you get your answers?

Working Smart, Not Hard

Just because you are working hard does not mean that you are getting things done. Working hard is the act of fooling yourself that you're moving forward when, in fact, you're just spinning your wheels. For example, if you have a job in sales, you might spend your time cleaning out your filing cabinet rather than making cold calls, or answering e-mails when you should be working on a report. By participating in similar acts of "busy-ness," you end your day feeling frustrated because you failed to achieve what you set out to do.

Working smart is putting a good system in place so you don't have to work so hard to achieve your goals. The key to working smart is making the most of your time by only doing activities that further your goals. Assess each activity. Delegate those that take you away from your goals. Add to your plan those activities that move you forward.

When working towards your goals, start small. Use small chunks of time to gain momentum. Most of us don't have large chunks of time to work on our careers. In reality, we can find fifteen minutes here, or one-half hour there. Seize these mini opportunities. If you spend fifteen minutes a day on one activity, in one year you'll have spent a grand total of ninety-one hours making your new career a reality!

Writing Exercise 7–3: Working Smart

1. What are your "work hard" activities?

2. How can you work smart instead?

3. What can you delegate?

4. What can you eliminate?

5. How can you manage your time better?

6. What process can you put in place in case you stray from your new system?

Having It All

Once you start gaining momentum, you may be tempted to immerse yourself in your goal. This is a good thing. But watch out. Goal achieving can be very addictive and can take over your life if you let it. If you sacrifice your health while pursuing your new career, all the achievements in the world won't matter. This is why maintaining balance is important for your overall well-being and that of the people around you. An easy way to accomplish this is to take time out one day or half a day each week to do whatever you want. Time just for you. This will allow you to entertain new ideas that, in turn, will give you energy to pursue your new career.

Writing Exercise 7–4: Fitting Your Career Choice Into Your Life

1. How will you maintain balance while you pursue your new career?

2. What measures will you take to not get carried away by your goal? For instance, will you schedule private time off?

Ask a friend, family member, mentor, or coach to help keep your life balanced. Allow this person to alert you if you about to go over the edge.

Affording Your New Career

"Can I really afford to do this?" "How am I going to pay the bills during my career transition?" I invite you to read the following comments from career changers who worried if they could afford their new career choices.

"I worried how I would be able to make a living and support my family. After getting a regular paycheck for 30+ years, I didn't know how I could go to a job that was 100% commission. I was determined not to give up. Getting my first listing after two months on the job and selling the house for full list price in five days put my fears to rest." Randall Livengood

"The hardest part was finding funding to pay for the courses I wanted to take. I had huge expenses with medical bills and paying off student loans for a career I no longer wanted to practice. I just kept saying that I would have what I wanted and pursued every avenue I could think of to get the money I needed. Push! Push! Push! I finally got the money, after searching and asking. I marketed myself tirelessly until I got what I wanted." Lenore Beck

"I was short on cash, but had faith and kept moving." Vicki Loveland

"I often thought that I could not afford to pursue a new career. I now know that I can't afford to NOT to pursue a new career." Sean North

"The main issue for me was finances. I was single and I had to pay my own bills. When I started getting positive feedback and payment from my clients, I thought if I just worked hard and kept this up, my new career could be a real success." Linda May

"Even though I worried a lot beforehand, I am better off financially, I am less stressed, and I feel more fulfilled because of my new career." Dale Alvaraz

Even after I decided that I wanted to be a coach, I didn't leave my high-paying job right away. I worked on my coaching practice for three and a half years in the evenings and weekends, until I had the financial means to go full time. Making a gradual transition into my new career allowed me to test the waters and assure its financial feasibility before taking the final step.

Writing Exercise 7–5: Assessing Your Finances

1. How much money do you make?

2. How much money do you owe?

3. Can any of your debt be refinanced?

4. What are your fixed expenses?

5. What are your discretionary expenses?

6. Which expenses can be eliminated or reduced?

7. What can you do to modify your lifestyle, if necessary?

8. What can you do to earn or save money to make your career goals a reality?

Some people have told me they refuse to give up their lifestyle even if their current career makes them miserable. I respect their choice and wouldn't try to convince them otherwise. But if your career drains every ounce of your energy and you've got that nagging feeling that you could be doing so much more with your life, ask yourself this: "What's more important? Where you live today or being happy tomorrow?" Only you can decide this.

Here's the truly uplifting story of Anne Wilson who quit her job and achieved financial freedom:

"In order for me to catch a glimpse of success, I first had to quit my day job. I know that doesn't sound like a practical thing to do, but in my case it became necessary.

"I was happiest in college when I was taking creative writing or literature, so what made me go into the field of court reporting? In one small word: MONEY. But after

17 years I was burnt out. In that field, there's no time for creative writing. Your days and nights are spent transcribing everybody else's voice. And I knew I had my voice inside me, screaming to get out.

"One day I was in the courtroom and the next day I was sitting at my computer at home. The first article that got published was On The Road To Castillo Di Santa Maria, a story about a charming castle I stayed at in Umbria, Italy. I was thrilled when a publisher called to say my story was going to be published.

"I continued to write. I wrote a story about my husband's Aunt Rose, Born on the Fourth of July, and it got published. Before I knew it, within three months of quitting my job, my articles and stories were showing up everywhere. I signed contracts with two newspapers. I am invigorated by my work.

"My thirst for writing overwhelms me. I love it! I'm blessed to have such a loving close family who supports my writing and love of artistic adventure."

Yes, you may experience an initial drop in income as you move into your new career, but in time your income will improve. I am not saying you have to quit your job to start a new career. I am saying do what feels right to you. You can take a part-time job or do some freelance work to make more money. Or you can save until you are ready to make your move. Whatever you choose, get your finances in order so when you are ready to begin your new career, money won't be the thing that stops you.

Your Support Team

I've observed that the number one reason people fail to make a career change is that they tried to do the change alone. In reality, few people can make any real change alone. Life isn't about overcoming obstacles or challenges on your own. It's about reaching goals with the help of other people. It may be tough to ask for assistance, but the rewards of reaching your goals with another person outweigh any embarrassment you may feel when asking for support.

Having the right support is crucial, according to these career changers:

"My best support came from my wife who constantly encouraged me. She reminded me that the success of our business does not dictate what makes me successful as a person." Dale Alvaraz

"My coach believed in me, pushed me, and became my biggest fan. Her support and affirmations made a tremendous difference in my life." Jelaine Gilliam

"My partner has given me tremendous support. From the little things like buying me a mug that says: Go confidently into the direction of your dreams, by Henry David Thoreau, to providing financial contributions in down times. I am very blessed." Anne Jenkins

"My current business partner supports my new direction. In fact, we're developing together a framework and strategy for my mission." Alex So

"I have one really good friend who is behind me 100%. She tells me that I'm brave and talented. She lets me complain, cry and be myself." Linda May

So, whose support can you enlist? Make a list of potential supporters, and start asking people to help you. Some people may refuse, but others will agree. There are people who want to help you. Let them.

8

The Finish Line

Reward Yourself

The best part of reaching your goal is the reward of a new career. This reward comes with a big bonus—the satisfaction of knowing that you can accomplish anything you want.

However, life's twists and turns may require you to spend more time on attaining your goal than you intended. This is why it's important to have little prizes for each milestone rather than rewarding yourself only at the finish line. This will keep your motivation and enthusiasm at its height, no matter what challenges you may face.

Writing Exercise 8–1: Planning Your Rewards

1. How will you reward yourself today for having the courage to go after your dreams?

2. What will be the reward for each milestone? (Set up some milestones if you have not done so already.)

3. What will be the big reward when you reach your goal?

Be Grateful

As you're learning and stumbling, count your blessings. Start a daily gratitude list. At the top of the page write, "I am grateful for" and each night record five things that you are grateful for. (This will make for pleasant dreams!)

Writing Exercise 8–2: What You Are Grateful For

1. Write down the five things you are grateful for.

2. If applicable, write down whom you are grateful for?

Cultivate your gratefulness and your success, and forward momentum will be yours forever.

Sharing Your Gift

The more successful you become, the more opportunities you have to share your gift of experience and knowledge with others. Sharing your gift is an act of appreciation that will keep your life and spirit balanced, and, in turn, you will receive more fulfillment than you could ever imagine.

Share your gift with the less fortunate who haven't yet achieved the ability to believe in their dreams. Be a role model who helps those who are just beginning to understand their potential. Be a person who makes a difference in the world! (This is why you switched careers to begin with, isn't it?)

If you wait to "arrive" before you share your gift, you may never share it. Look for opportunities needed along your journey and it will feed your enthusiasm along the way.

Writing Exercise 8–3: The Gift You Will Share

1. How will you share your gift?

2. Who will keep you accountable for this promise?

Keep Improving

"Every day, in every way, I am getting better and better." **Emile Coue**

Don't stop just because you are in your new career. Strive to improve constantly. This will keep you on your toes.

Check in with yourself monthly for areas you can improve. Use mistakes as learning experiences to advance and develop. If you stumble, pick yourself up and keep going. Don't be intimidated by your mistakes, failures, or embarrassments. Instead, use them to build up your treasure trove of experience.

Writing Exercise 8–4: The Improvements You Will Make

1. How will you strive to improve after you reach your goal?

2. Who will keep you accountable for this promise?

Conclusion

You have made remarkable progress You have shown tremendous courage by examining your career and creating a plan towards making your new career choice real. You have discovered that you are the navigator of your career, your dreams, and your happiness. Notice how you feel now compared to how you felt when you first started this book. Congratulations, this is a milestone. Remember to reward yourself!

Here are a few happy endings that will inspire you:

"My new career is absolutely the best thing that has ever happened to me." Randall Livengood, downsized human resources manager, 24 years with the same company, turned successful realtor

"I know that I am a good example for our son and a better wife to my husband as a result of pursing a career I am passionate about." Jennifer Carlson, formerly in sales turned social worker

"I have less stress in my life. I'm happier and my kids are happier. I haven't doubted my decision for a second." Julie Raque, former advertising account manager, turned success coach and public speaker

"I have this interior sense of excitement and calmness, happening at the same time. I am finally doing it!" Linda May, laid off full-time employee turned business owner and entrepreneur

"I am more creative now. I am open to opportunities, possibilities, and am responsible for the results I produce in my life and the lives of other people. I am a person who is making a positive contribution in the world." Anne Jenkins, former office administrator turned freelance professional

"I have made moves, and done things that I would have never done before. I understand my true worth and am confident in my actions. I am finally able to be me." Lenore Beck, former sales trainer, manager, and business owner turned coach

"Today, I am independent and not afraid of anything. I've learned that where there is a will, there is a way, and I have found that way." Vicki Loveland, former legal assistant turned writer/singer

Where They See Themselves Five Years From Now

"In five years, I will be running a successful healing art business, having three successful residual income sources, being well off with my investments, traveling around the world, and helping people make the shift from financial to spiritual evolution." Rey White, investor

"In five years, I will be an owner of a thriving business and surrounded by people who love me. Life will keep getting better as I see the results of my efforts continue to grow." Dale Alvaraz, investor/business owner/consultant

"In five years, I will be well into my new career and will have helped a lot of people put their lives back into order. I'll have a thankful heart because I am making a difference in the world." Sarah Davidson, senior care officer, United Kingdom

Marianne Williamson, internationally acclaimed author and lecturer, wrote the following:

Our deepest fear is not that we are inadequate. Our deepest fear is that we are powerful beyond measure. It is our light, not our darkness that most frightens us. And as we let our own light shine, we unconsciously give other people permission to do the same. As we are liberated from our own fear, our presence automatically liberates others.[1]

You are smart and talented and have unique gifts to give to the world. You are special and you have a purpose for being alive. Go out there and be the person you were meant to be. You are ready. You can do it. I know you can.

---

1. From *A Return To Love: Reflections on the Principles of A Course in Miracles,* Harper Collins, 1992, (from Chapter 7, Section 3), by Marianne Williamson.

APPENDIX A

About The Author

Deborah Brown-Volkman

I am the president and founder of Surpass Your Dreams, Inc., a career and mentor coaching company that has been delivering a message of motivation, success, and personal fulfillment since 1998. We work Senior Executives, Vice Presidents, and Managers who are out of work or overworked. We also work with Coaches who want to build profitable coaching practices.

Current and former clients include individuals from: JPMorganChase, Oracle Corporation, Lucent Technologies, General Motors, Procter & Gamble, Ziff Davis, IBM, American Express, EDS, Ogilvy & Mather, McCann-Erickson Worldgroup, Columbia University, New York University, Chief Executive Magazine, MSNBC, and BMW.

I am a published writer, and my articles on how to be successful in your career can be found on more than 100 web sites. I am the author of an e-book titled *Living A Life You Love! The Pathway to Personal Freedom* that can help you discover your ideal career by discovering yourself first. I write a monthly e-mail newsletter and weekly tips titled *Surpass Your Dreams* that offers practical advice and steps so Monday can be the best day of the work week.

I have been quoted as a career expert by the *Wall Street Journal*, the *New York Times*, *Smart Money Magazine*, and *New York Newsday*, as well as having been interviewed by *Entrepreneur Magazine* and *Business 2.0*. I was also a featured guest on BBC, Radio Scotland when they came to New York City to find out how people were coping in their careers since the September 11th attacks.

I am a graduate of Coach University's Coaches Program, an accredited program for business & personal coaching, and am enrolled in Coachville's Graduate School Of Coaching. I also am the president and the founder of the *United Coaching Associates*, a founding member of Coachville.com, and a member of the International Coach Federation.

Before becoming a coach, I spent twelve years managing sales and marketing programs for Fortune 500 companies and dot.coms. I received an A.A.S. degree in data processing from Queensborough Community College, a B.A. in marketing from Hofstra University, and a certificate in financial planning from New York University.

My husband Brian and I live in Long Island, NY.

For additional information, you can contact me at http://www. surpassyourdreams.com or by e-mail at info@surpassyourdreams.com

Appendix B
Additional Career Articles

As a bonus, I have included five of my most popular career articles. I put them into the book to motivate and inspire you go after what you want in your career.

Are You In The Wrong Career?

Are you happy when you come to work in the morning, or happy when it is time to go home? Do you look forward to Friday, and then get knots in your stomach on Sunday evenings? If this is the case, there is probably nothing wrong with you physically. You may be in the wrong career.

Most people view their lives as being separate parts: work life/social life/home life. Your life has many components, but when you are in the wrong career, the rest of your life is out of balance.

So How Do You Know If You Are In The Wrong Career? Ask Yourself The Following:

1. Do I Have A Hard Time Falling Asleep At Night?

Are you so wound up at the end of the day that you cannot seem to calm down at night? If you are playing the same thoughts in your head over and over again, you are probably trying to get closure for the day. You could also be trying to make sense of what is happening around you. If you were in the right career, you would fall asleep easier.

2. Do I Have Trouble Making It To Work On Time?

Most of the time, being late does not happen by accident. Yes, outside circumstance could be the reason you are not getting to work on time, but your lateness is probably a result of your not wanting to be there. If you were in the right career, you would make it to work on time.

3. Do I Feel Rundown?

Have you put on weight recently? Stopped exercising? Do you get frequent headaches, stomachaches, or colds? All are telltale signs that your career is taking away from your quality of life. If you were in the right career, you would not be punishing your body.

4. Do I Wish I Were Somewhere Else?

If you wish you were somewhere else, then it may be time to make a plan to get yourself there. There does not have to be anything wrong with you for wanting something different. If your inner voice is screaming for more, it may be time to listen. If you were in the right career, you might think about doing something else, but not all the time.

5. Do I Believe That There Is Nothing I Can Do About My Situation?

When you are in the wrong career, you lose the ability to see a way out. You become consumed with your unhappiness and forget that something is better around the corner. If you were in the right career, your thinking would be clear.

DID YOU THINK YOU WOULD BE SOMEWHERE ELSE IN YOUR CAREER BY NOW?

Do you love what you do? Or do you spend your time thinking back to the jobs you turned down, or to the paths you could have taken?

The past is called the past because it is in the past. The decisions you made, or did not make, may have taught you some tough lessons, but you can use these lessons to build a brighter future. You get to say how your future will go, and you get to choose where you will end up. Release yourself of past mistakes.

Maybe your current career choice was your best choice at the time that you made it. Maybe you made a wrong turn (it happens to all of us!) but either way there is still time to get back on track if you want to. It really does not matter how old you are, what gender you are, where you live, your education, or how much money you have. Nothing can get in the way of a person who is willing to try.

So How Do You Make Peace With Where You Are Today So You Can Create A New Future? Follow These Steps:

1. Get To Know Yourself Better

The more you know yourself, the better you will be able to decide what is best for you. It is easy to make decisions when you know what's right for you vs. trying to make decisions based on what others think you should do. You will be swayed less by choices that do not work for you and will lean more towards choices that do work for you, if you know what your values and goals are first.

2. Forgive Others

Your family, friends, colleagues, bosses, etc. meant well in their advice to you. Their intentions may have been influenced by what they wanted, but trust that they meant no harm. They really do want the best for you. When you forgive others, the blame disappears, and you get your life back. You free yourself up to take responsibility for your own choices, and what your future will look like.

3. Forgive Yourself

Do you believe you have to be perfect? Allow yourself to make mistakes and learn from them. You are human and human beings have flaws. (Your life would be boring without them.) Forgive yourself and then promise that you will make different choices going forward. People get second chances everyday. So can you.

4. Trust Your Instinct

The career that is right for you is within you. But back when you made the first choice in your career, fear may have kept you from taking the path you really wanted to take. Today, it may be bills that are keeping you in the same place. Trust your instinct (the little voice inside that tells you your true purpose in life), and you can get your dream career.

5. Recognize That It Is Not Too Late

There will always be a reason not to push ahead and try something new. But the alternative of not venturing out is having a career you do not love. My mom who is 56 has just gone back to school and sometimes she is the oldest person is the classroom. She tells me that this is not a deterrent because she would not want to be anywhere else. If you tell yourself that it is too late, then it will be. How about telling yourself that there is plenty of time?

6. Get A Plan

Decide that it is important to live a life without regrets. Then, set goals to support this decision. Goals help you focus your efforts and motivate you to move forward. You can get always get a job, but a job you love requires planning.

7. Take A Chance

It all comes down to "will you do it or will you not?" Life grants big rewards, but only to those who put in the work first. Step out of your comfort zone and out of your own way. Take a chance. You can do it.

ARE YOU ATTACHED TO HOW IT IS SUPPOSED TO TURN OUT?

Is there a career goal you have been shooting for that has not come to fruition? Are you frustrated and confused because it is taking so long? Do you wonder when you will see the results of your hard work?

Maybe the problem is that you are attached to how it is supposed to turn out.

When you focus solely on the end result, you miss out on the opportunity to enjoy today. When you wait until one day in the future to be happy, you are unable to appreciate where you are now.

You also lose sight of the reason you choose your goal to begin with. You started with wanting to enhance your career, and after a while, your goal seemed like drudgery. Drudgery creeps in when you are no longer choosing your goal, and allowing your goal to choose you.

So How Do You Achieve Your Goal Without Focusing Solely On The Result?

1. Recognize What The Attachment Is Costing You

There is no fun when you are only living for the future. Yes, a new career or a promotion can make you smile, but can you honestly say you have been the easiest person to be around these days?

2. Accept Where You Are Today

What's wrong with where you are? Just because you have not achieved what you want in your career today, does not mean you will not achieve it tomorrow. Let go of the yearning, and immerse yourself in the here and now.

3. Let Go Of The Result

Imagine the room you will have to be yourself again when you let go of having to obtain your goal right now. This thought could be unsettling if you do not know who you would be if you were not clinging to your goal. Think about how much freedom you will have when it does not matter what happens. And who knows, this freedom might give you the burst of energy you have been looking for to get what you want.

4. Choose Your Goal All Over Again

Now that you have let go of how it should turn out, you can re-choose your goal. Remember when you first said you wanted a change? It was freeing, right? Then somewhere down the road it wasn't liberating anymore. Choose your career goal because you want to. Not because you should, or you think you have to, but because it will enhance the quality of your life.

5. Trust That It Will All Work Out

If all things work out in the end (and they usually do), then why all the worry? Trust that you are on the right path. Trust that you are headed in the right direction. Trust that you will have what you want in your career. Be happy even if the result you want does not arrive right now.

PRETEND THAT YOU COULD SEE YOURSELF ONE YEAR FROM NOW

Imagine a year has gone by. It was a taxing time in your career, but it was well worth it, because you are now enjoying your career tremendously. You are grateful for what transpired over the past year. If it were not for that difficulty, you would not be where you are today.

It took you a while to find your way, but you have arrived. You battled fear, uncertainty, and yourself. But you have come out a winner. Looking back, you see that there were five key steps that were your crucial to your success. They were:

1. You Accepted Where You Were

You stopped blaming the world for your predicament. You decided to forgive those who caused your situation. Most importantly, you forgave yourself. You acknowledged where you were because you knew that a better tomorrow would not happen until you accepted today.

2. You Decided You Would Win

You realized that you worked too hard to get where you were in your career, and you were not going to give up. You also decided that your present situation would not get the best of you. You let go of the shoulds, and the reasons why you couldn't have what you wanted in your career. Then you made a plan to go after what you truly deserved.

3. You Persevered

You had a vision in your mind, and you did not give up. Sure, there were obstacles. But, you woke up each morning and told yourself that today was a brand new day. You made phone calls you were afraid to make. You wrote e-mails and letters you weren't sure would get read. You went to meetings and seminars, and you networked. But most importantly, you were afraid and you moved forward anyway.

4. You Asked For Help

This was a big deal for you because you were used to doing things on your own. You opened yourself up and asked for what you needed. You were surprised and appreciative because people from unexpected places took the time to help you. The best thing you learned is that life is much easier when you are not reaching your goals alone.

5. You Knew You Would End Up In A Better Place

You stopped driving yourself crazy because you knew things would improve. You recognized that your situation was only temporary. As a result, you enjoyed yourself more. You spent time getting to know you again. You lost weight or took up a new hobby. You tried new things, and you grew in ways you never imagined possible. You are so much stronger and wiser now. You are not the same.

CAREER DISTRESS? BEING INSPIRED IS YOUR ANSWER.

Many people I speak with are looking for that magic formula, the recipe that will transform their careers. The truth is they may never find what they are looking for. The reason is they are looking outward, when the answer is within.

I've seen many individuals create amazing careers. Even when they are told there are no jobs, or they'll never make the career transition they want, they are still securing positions that they love. How are they doing it? They are inspired.

Inspiration is that almighty force that arises from the inside. It lights you up and gives you more power that you ever expected. Think about a time in your career when you were excited and energized because everything was going your way. Can you imagine being able to apply that feeling to where you are today?

What Will You Do Differently If You Are Inspired?

1. You Will Call The Person You've Been Afraid To Call

You will find yourself picking up the telephone and having conversations with people that get them excited. You will be able to articulate exactly what you want, and be amazed as the person on the other end extends a hand to help you.

2. You Will Send The E-Mail You've Been Afraid Of Sending

You will stop telling yourself that people are too overwhelmed to read your e-mail. You will write e-mails that inspire people to take action, and they will. Your creativity will be at its height, and your words will flow easily.

3. You Will Send The Letters You've Been Afraid To Send

You will find yourself buying the finest paper so your words can stand out. You will find the addresses of the people you want to contact effortlessly. The people to whom you write will read your letters because they will want to know more about the passionate person who wrote them.

4. You Will Meet The People You've Been Afraid To Meet

You will get out and network with the people you have been staying away from. You will find yourself describing what you want eloquently and the people you speak with will understand you and refer you to someone who can assist you. You will enjoy yourself and be comfortable in the surroundings of people you do not know. People will want to know who you are, and your magnetism will be the catalyst that creates the relationship.

5. You Will Have The Conversations You've Been Afraid To Have

You will speak to the people in your life and ask for the support you need to move forward. You will apologize and take responsibility for expecting them to read your mind. You will acknowledge them for the gift they have been in your life. You will tell them what you want and why it is important that you receive it from them. They will appreciate your honesty and provide you with the assistance you need.

6. You Will Conquer Your Fears

And your life will never be the same.

So, how do you get inspired? You put your disappointments behind you because you realize how much they are holding you back. You recognize that your career gets better when you make it better. You write down your vision on a piece of paper, and you look at it every day. Then you put a plan in place to get it.

Appendix C

The Progress Report

It's always a good idea to check in every once in a while to make sure you are on track. Use this form each month to track your progress.

<u>Answer The Following Questions:</u>

1. The dreams I identified and turned into goals were:

2. In the past month, I have accomplished the following steps:

3. I am really proud of myself for:

4. I am rewarding myself by:

5. My action plan for the next month is as follows:

Congratulations on your dedication, momentum, and courage. You have made great strides!

0-595-29658-0

Printed in the United States
73118LV00004B/230

9 780595 296583